The Christmas STORY

This is the true story of what happened
at the very first Christmas and why it happened.
The Christmas that most of us know about is
only good news during the holiday season.
The *real* story of Christmas is good news
for every day of our lives.

J.JOHN

Illustrated by Morena Forza

The first Christmas didn't just happen by accident. It happened for a reason, and to understand that reason we need to go back a long, long way.

The Bible tells us that in the beginning everything in the world was very good. God made people to be friends with him and with each other. He put them in a beautiful garden with everything they needed.

Sadly, things went wrong.
The first people, Adam and Eve, decided
they wanted to run their lives their own way,
not God's way. They had to leave their garden
paradise and soon God seemed far away.
And the world was broken without God.

But God still loved everybody and was very sad about what had happened. He decided to do something about it and chose a man called Abraham.

God promised Abraham that through his children he would help to fix the world. Over many years, Abraham's descendants became the Jewish people and lived in Israel, the land that God had given them.

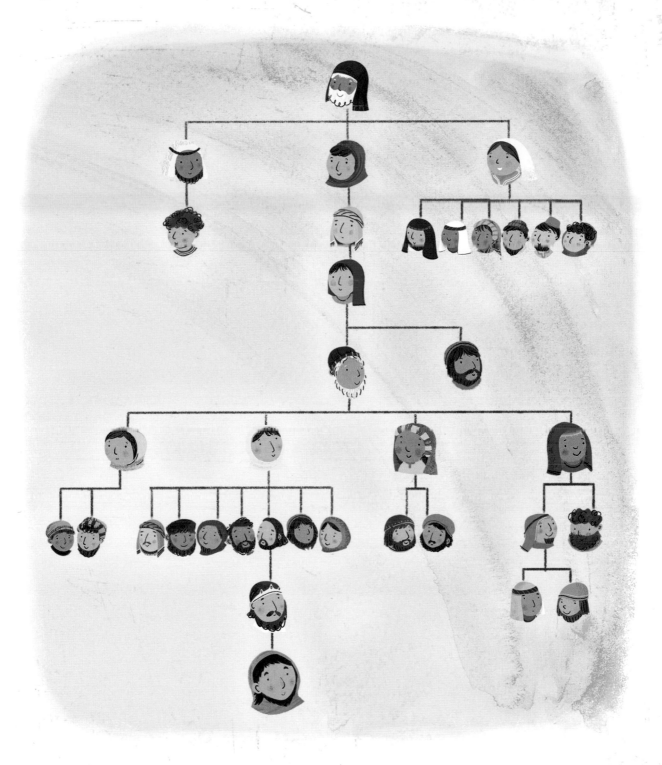

Time passed. God's people kept getting into trouble but God always rescued them. He sent messengers to remind them who he was and to guide them back to him.

In order to protect and lead his people, God gave them kings. The greatest and best of those kings was David from a place called Bethlehem.

In time people built a big temple where they could be closer to God. But despite the messengers, the kings and the temple, God still seemed far away.

God made many promises to his people that one day a special king would come who would bring God and people back together again. The Jewish people kept waiting for a child to be born who would be the promised king.

Finally, two thousand years ago, things began to happen...

The first thing that happened was that an angel appeared to an old man called Zechariah who served in the temple. The angel told him that, after a lifetime of waiting, his wife Elizabeth would have a baby son.

This boy would be someone special: he would be filled with God's Holy Spirit and would prepare the way for God's king.

The baby was to be called John. Later in the Bible we read how John made people ready for God's king by baptising them in water as a sign that their sins had been washed away and their lives were clean.

But the really important thing was what happened at almost the same time in a town called Nazareth.

A young girl called Mary lived there and she loved God. Mary was engaged to be married to a man called Joseph.

One day she was visited by an angel called Gabriel.
'Don't be afraid, Mary. God is pleased with you,' Gabriel
said. 'You are going to become pregnant. The boy you
will have will be called Jesus and he will be great.'

The name Jesus means 'God rescues' and *rescuing* is
exactly what Jesus does. 'People will call Jesus the
Son of God,' Gabriel continued, 'and he will be a king
like David, only with a kingdom that will never end.'

Mary didn't understand. 'There's a problem,' she said. 'You need a man to produce babies and Joseph and I aren't yet married.'

Gabriel replied, 'That isn't a problem for God. The baby will be made through God's Holy Spirit.'

This tells us that Jesus was not going to be an ordinary human being like you or me, but God as well.

Mary bowed her head. 'I am God's servant. May your promises come true.'

She was so filled with joy that she sang a song to God praising him for what he was doing for his people.

Joseph was not happy when he heard that the girl he was going to marry was pregnant. But he had a dream in which an angel spoke to him, telling him not to worry; Mary had done nothing wrong and the baby who was coming had been made by the Holy Spirit.

You might have expected that Mary would stay in Nazareth to have her baby but God had other plans.

At this time Israel was controlled by the powerful Roman Empire, ruled by Caesar Augustus.

He needed more people to pay money to the government in taxes, so he ordered everybody to go back to where they came from so that they could be registered for tax.

As Joseph was descended from King David and came from Bethlehem, that was where he had to go. He took Mary with him.

It was a long journey and when Mary and Joseph got to Bethlehem they found that there was nowhere for them to stay.

The only place they could find was a room where animals were kept. This was where Jesus was born, and Mary and Joseph wrapped him up and put him in a cattle trough.

How very strange that when the King who will rule forever came to earth he was born in such a poor little place!

Bethlehem was a village in the countryside surrounded by fields where shepherds were looking after their flocks of sheep.

That night an angel appeared to the shepherds in a dazzling blaze of light. They were terrified!

The angel told them not to be afraid. 'I'm bringing you good news,' he said. 'The one who will save the world, the baby who will become a greater king than David, has been born in Bethlehem. You will find him in a cattle trough.'

And with that the night sky opened to show thousands of angels praising God.

After the angels had disappeared back into heaven, the shepherds rushed off to Bethlehem to find the baby. Then they returned to their sheep, singing praises to God and telling everybody about what they had seen.

The way that God told the shepherds to come to see the baby reminds us that Jesus came to earth for all of us, whether we are rich or poor.

When Jesus was just a few days old Mary and Joseph took him to the great temple in Jerusalem.

To their surprise two people at the temple realised who Jesus was. One was a very old man called Simeon. He told Mary and Joseph that the child would be a light to show God to the whole world.

A wise woman called Anna recognised that the baby would grow up to be the king who would rescue God's people.

The shepherds were not the only visitors to see Jesus.
Far away to the east of Israel were some wise men
who studied the stars.

These wise men noticed an unusual star in the sky
that showed them that a king had been born to the
Jewish people. So they prepared precious gifts and
began a long journey to try to find him.

Now at this time Israel wasn't just ruled by the Romans but also a king called Herod. He was nasty and cruel. He was always worrying that someone would come to take his throne away from him.

The wise men from the east went straight to King Herod's palace expecting to find the baby there. When they explained why they had come, Herod became jealous that this baby might be God's king.

Because he was an evil man he pretended that he wanted to find the baby so he could pay his respects. He sent the wise men to Bethlehem with instructions to come back and tell him where the baby could be found. But he didn't want to take presents to Jesus; he just wanted to kill him.

Guided by the star the wise men found where baby Jesus was.

They were delighted and, opening their treasure chests, gave him gifts of gold, sweet-smelling frankincense and a spicy ointment called myrrh.

The way that God told the wise men to come to see the baby reminds us that Jesus came to earth for everybody, wherever we come from.

As the wise men were planning to return to their own country, God warned them not to go near Herod. So, without him noticing, they slipped quietly away.

As they left, an angel came to Joseph and warned him that Herod was going to search for Jesus to kill him. Without waiting, Joseph took Mary and Jesus and left for Egypt where they would be safe from Herod.

Eventually, much to everyone's relief, King Herod died. Mary, Joseph and the young Jesus returned to Nazareth where Jesus grew up. But those who knew the story of his birth wondered what was going to happen to him.

So that's *how* Jesus was born.

The Bible also tells us *why* he was born. It says that Jesus was 'God with us'. Remember how, long, long ago, people had turned away from God and become separated from him? Jesus was not just an ordinary baby; he was God coming to be one of us. We couldn't get back to God so he came to be with us.

Many years later we have the Easter story when Jesus died on a cross so we could all be forgiven. And then Jesus rose from the dead and returned to heaven. Although Jesus is now in heaven he is still 'God with us'.

Because of the first Christmas, Jesus can be with us today to help us, guide us and protect us. If you would like God to be with you, pray this prayer:

Dear Father in heaven, thank you for giving us
Jesus, the greatest Christmas gift of all.
Thank you, Jesus, for being born on earth
and dying on the cross for me.

Please come into my life so I may know
your presence and peace. Please make my life
clean and new. Please help me, guide me
and protect me. Help me to follow you.

Thank you for your love for me.
May I be a shining example
of your love to others.

Amen.